How I Work with ANGELS

Matthew Robert Payne

This book is copyrighted by Matthew Robert Payne. Copyright © 2021. All rights reserved.

Any part of this book can be photocopied, stored, or shared with anyone for the purposes of encouraging people. You are free to quote this book, use whole chapters of this book on blog posts, or use this book to spread the message of Jesus with this world. No consent from the author is required of you. If multiple copies of the paperback are needed for outreach, please contact the author for wholesale rates.

Please visit http://personal-prophecy-today.com to sow into Matthew's writing ministry, to request a personal prophecy or other prophetic services. You can read up to 38 books online for free written by Matthew Robert Payne at https://matthewrobertpayne.com

Cover designed by akira007 at https://www.fiverr.com

All Scripture is taken from the New King James Version unless otherwise noted. Copyright © 1982 by Thomas Nelson, Inc. Used by permission. All rights reserved.

Scripture quotations marked (NLT) are taken from the Holy Bible, New Living Translation, copyright ©1996, 2004, 2007, 2013, 2015 by Tyndale House Foundation. Used by permission of Tyndale House Publishers, Inc., Carol Stream, Illinois 60188. All rights reserved.

The opinions expressed by the author are not necessarily those of RWG Publishing. Published by RWG Publishing. RWG Publishing is committed to excellence in the publishing industry. Book design Copyright © 2020 by RWG Publishing. All rights reserved.

Paperback ISBN: 978-1-64830-271-8

Dedication

This book is dedicated to all of those hungry hearts who hope one day to work with angels and those who already have had to good fortune to do so.

Special Note about Editing

In times past in most of my books that have been published previously I had a very expensive editor that I used to edit my books. My ministry income has now halved, and I cannot afford the expense for that quality of editor, so I apologize that the quality of my writing has decreased. I hope that you can appreciate my predicament and that you will still choose to read my books. If you "feel led." to sponsor the editing for a future book with a higher quality of editing, I would be open to that.

Table of Contents

Dedication iii

Special note about Editing v

Introduction 1

Meeting Jonathan 5

Vote in Israel 11

Jonathan speaks 13

Meeting Mark—A Finance Angel 17

Mark speaks 21

Matthew speaks 27

Bethany's effect in my life 29

Bethany, a scribe angel, speaks 31

Meeting Michael—My Guardian Angel 35

Michael the guardian angel speaks 41

The effect of Michael the Archangel on my life 45

Michael the Archangel speaks 47

Let's talk about Gamiel the Archangel 55

Gamiel speaks 59

Commanding angels 63

Guardian Angel messages 67

Satan's portal in my house 71

The effect of thousands of angels walking in the glory 73
Katrina speaks 75
New story 77
Postscript 78
Important contact 78
Closing thoughts 79
I'd Love to Hear from You 81
How to Sponsor a Book Project 83
About Matthew Robert Payne 85
Acknowledgments 87

Introduction

I hope to make this a small book. I hope that it's interesting for people. I have a book called *My Radical Encounters with Angels* and I have a book called *My Radical Encounters with Angels: Book Two*. They have a lot of angel stories in them, and I hope that you enjoy some of the stories in this book.

This book's focus is going to be a lot more on ministering with angels, and specifically the effect of ministering with angels. It's possible to meet angels from time to time. You can have a Christian life where you meet angels in a vision, or you meet angels in the flesh. That's fine—angels have got their reasons for turning up and they've got their reasons for existing.

Angels all come on assignment. There is a very interesting book called *Angels on Assignment* which shows you that angels do appear on assignment. But I want to give a note in this short introduction and share with you that if you run after angels, if you get to meet angels and your purpose is a fascination with angels, then you're going to run into familiar spirits and demonic interference. If you have an overt interest in angels and you are not grounded in God, you're going to have issues with counterfeit angels. This is simply because in order to effectively minister with angels, and effectively have a good relationship with them, you've got to have intimacy with Jesus. Jesus has got to be your focal point and the reason why you're living. If Jesus isn't your closest friend, and if you haven't got an intimate relationship with Jesus, then encountering angels is almost idolatry.

There's nothing grand about angels. Angels are servants that are meant to serve God and minister to us, but they're not amazing celebrities that you need to meet. They're not something to be sought after or worshipped in any way. I find that the world has a fascination with angels. I did a couple of angel books a few years ago. It's taken me until now to actually do a third angel book, even though my first angel book, *My Radical Encounters with Angels*, is the best-selling book I've ever had. It's sold a whole lot of copies, and so it's tempting to keep on writing angel books. But I've realized that people have an unhealthy fascination with angels, and my message is Jesus and obedience to Jesus. So, please pay attention to developing intimacy with Jesus. I want the focus of this book to be about how angels have been used to minister in my life and in ministering the Word of God to the people that I touch. They were part of the messages that I preach through Facebook and through videos on YouTube, and that I've preached in my books. I really want to make clear, and help people to understand, that my focus is solely on Jesus.

I exist to promote the name of Jesus and His ways, His dictates, the things He commands, and the things that He preached. I've got a couple of pages' worth of notes here which will be my chapter headings, and I'm going to slowly go through them. I'm not going to say too much to extend the time. I'm just going to read the chapter headings and say what I feel needs to be said under each heading and each section and then I'll go on. I'm not going to say a lot to make it a longer book for the sake of it; I'm just going to say what needs to be said.

Note: This book was transcribed from a video that I recorded and edited, so it differs from the original video now. If I mention the word 'video' or the fact that this message is a video, please be aware that I have not edited that out. Also, please note that there will be virtually no quotes of Bible verses to support what I have written in this book. If you want scriptural support for the ministry of angels, there are plenty of dry books for that. There are heaps of strangers speaking on behalf of a supposed God that they serve to cleverly back up their lies with scripture. This is the life I live and what I have personally experienced, and you should be a good Berean and search out evidence for yourself in the scriptures if anything makes you doubt me. You can always ask the Holy Spirit to confirm this message with His anointing and peace.

Matthew Robert Payne

Meeting Jonathan

I have a friend called Auty. I have Auty's website listed at the back of this book. Auty said prophetically that I was going to get a spiritual promotion. I ordered a prophetic blueprint from Auty, which is something that talks about your destiny, your destiny scroll, and the purpose that you have on Earth. Auty can provide one of them for $120 USD. I ordered one because I was interested in the purpose of my life. In the midst of the prophetic blueprint, he said that I was going to get a promotion—I was going to get an angelic company to come and join me. I will say something about Auty and his prophetic gift: I've never met anyone whose prophetic gift is so in tune with 'now words' (a now word is a prophetic word that manifests straightaway in your life). I've encountered a number of Auty's prophetic words and they manifest straightaway.

When he said I was going to get an angelic promotion, it was fresh in my mind. Half an hour later, I left my house. As I left my house, I saw 2,000 angelic commanders aligning in my street. I'd seen these 2,000 commanders before. Each of the commanders is in charge of 3,000 angels. So, the 2,000 commanders are in charge of 6 million angels total. Only the commanders appear to you—the 6 million angels are all there, but you only see the commander in charge of them. So, I was walking through all of the commanders and Auty had said that I would deal with one commander for all the angels, and he would introduce himself to me. I walked down the street and walked to another street and the whole street was full of commanding angels.

As I sat down, I asked, "What's your name?" I sensed an angel next to me.

He said, "My name is Jonathan."

I said, "You're the commander of these 6 million angels?"

"Yeah, I am."

I said, "I've seen these 2,000 angels before. I've used them and dispatched them before. So, when I dispatched them before, I was dispatching you?

Jonathan said, "Yes, that's true."

I asked, "So you're with me permanently now?"

"Yes, that's true," he replied.

So, I had a conversation with him, and he presented his name as Jonathan. I want to make the point that some people give accounts of meeting angels and they don't know the angel's name. I've found personally that I've been able to get the name of every angel I've met, and I've been able to communicate with them. Perhaps that's my intimacy with Jesus; perhaps that's where I'm stationed in the Lord's heart. One thing I know is that angels have assignments and permissions—just like software has certain permissions and certain people that can access certain programs. Unless you've got permission to have the software, you can't go to certain parts of it; you need the proper clearance, like you see in spy movies that people have to have a certain clearance to access a certain part of the software.

The same happens with angels. Depending on who you are in God, depending on your intimacy with the Father and Jesus, they have things they can allow or not allow. Angels have certain permissions. So, it's possible for an angel to turn up and comfort you, but they are not allowed to talk to you or converse with you. You may just be able to see the angel. It's possible for an angel to turn up but you're not able to get the angel's name. There's power in a name, and maybe they don't want you to access the power. But that's never been the case for me.

Another thing that's different with me is that I've never seen an angel and been scared. I've never been in fear of an angel. The fear of God has never come over me, no matter which angel I've met. Many books on angels (and I love books on angels from Christians, too) disclose that they were in great fear and they fell down at the presence. They were in shock and reverent fear of the Lord. This has never happened to me with angels, it's never happened to me with God, and it's never happened to me with Jesus. I've met God in heaven; I've met God on Earth. I've met Jesus in heaven; I've met Jesus on Earth. In fact, I've met Jesus in the flesh 10 times. I've never fallen down in fear. Once again, I feel it must be my relationship with God. It depends on your relationship.

Let me go on with the story. I've got Jonathan's name. I know Jonathan was there. That was a Wednesday afternoon. It was the 15th of May, 2019.

I said to Jonathan, "You're in charge of 6 million angels?"

He said, "Yeah."

I said, "Can I do a test with you?"

He said, "Sure."

I said, "Can you go and speak to all the undecided voters in Australia, and all the people who are voting Labor (which is Australia's Democratic Party)? Can you go to all the people who haven't decided which party to vote for? Go to all the people that can be swayed in the Labor Party. Can you get them to vote for our Conservative Party (which is our Liberal Party)?"

He said, "Sure."

I said, "So can you win this election for us?"

He said, "I'll do my best."

Jonathan went off on the Wednesday, and the election was on Saturday the 19th of May. It wasn't til I was having lunch on Sunday that I saw the news on TV. Australia had a miracle election. It was even called "a miracle"—there was a three- to four-point swing against the Labor Party. The Conservative Party were definitely, according to the polls, not meant to win. They were saying that it was a Trump-like win, and I knew that Jonathan had swayed the election for me.

Now, I want to give you some understanding here. It wasn't just sending Jonathan out to speak to people—it was the 6 million angels. You've got to understand, or perhaps you don't and that's why I'm explaining. You're going to have to understand the mechanics of angels.

If you look at the history of angels in the Bible (and this book isn't going to be replete with scriptures on angels), you'll see often that angels met with people, but they met with people in a dream. A dream state is a really good way to receive information. So, what I had Jonathan do, and I've done this before in angelic dispatches, is I had Jonathan's angels go into the dream of a person. Then, one of the 6 million angels appeared as their best friend and started to have a conversation about the upcoming election—why they're voting for the Conservative Party and why their friend should vote for the Conservative Party. The angel pretended to be their friend, or the actual guardian angel of their friend could appear to them. Jonathan may have commissioned guardian angels to do that.

There were a couple of dreams; there were two different-looking friends appearing on consecutive nights speaking to their friend and sharing why they should vote Conservative. So, they had consistent dreams about the election. Angels spoke to them, but the angels looked like one of their friends, or their daughter, or someone that they knew, and said to them, "You should really vote for the Conservative Party." So, when the election came, there was a swing because there had been some major advertising done through the angelic. That's how to minister with angels.

That mission was not the first mission on which I have sent the 6 million angels. It's not until you're given 6 million angels and have done several jobs that you learn how to do it. So, I sent these angels out and they turned the Australian election. Why did I have them vote for the Conservative Party? Number one is because I don't believe in abortion. Even during this Australian government's term, they approved of increased abortion laws. But the other reason I wanted the Conservative Party in is because they promised to build more stadiums. For the outpouring and revival before Jesus comes, we're going to need stadiums built for stadium revivals. This party promised to build stadiums, so I was used through Jonathan to swing the election.

Vote in Israel

Later, in September that year, Israel had an election. I'm not sure if it was a parliamentary election or a presidential election. I sent Jonathan to go and deal with that too and to speak in their dreams. That had a surprising turnaround too, and an unexpected result. So, you can see what I'm saying is true and can really happen. I can command 6 million angels, and they're happy to carry out my command. Of course, the angels will only do the will of God and what has been prayed for by the people, so one prerequisite to commanding angels is your ability to be led by the Holy Spirit in all that you do and say. It's important to have an understanding of how to command angels.

So that was Jonathan, and he helped turn the Australian election and then an election in Israel.

The angels bring a fresh anointing into my life. I'm going to have Jonathan speak for a little while now. Most of this book is going to be about an angel in my life, and then I'm going to have the angel speak. As a seer and a prophet, I can take on the voice of someone else. Jonathan's going to speak through me, and he's a commanding angel who's responsible for the 6 million angels that are attached to my ministry. I've got authority according to the leading of the Holy Spirit to have them do anything I choose. So, we'll just let Jonathan speak.

Jonathan speaks

It's great to talk to you, and it's great for you to be watching this video or reading this book. It's a very humbling experience to speak to humans; we regard humans very highly. We definitely regard people who are humble and are great servants of the Lord in high favor.

We really admire Matthew, and we admire people whose whole lives are dedicated to Jesus Christ. Matthew didn't get my service from nothing. He's always had a great understanding of angels, and he's always had a good relationship with them. Throughout his life, he's met many angels and he's been respectful and humble. There's a scripture in the Bible that says that humans are going to command angels and judge angels, but Matthew has never been interested in judging angels or demons. He's got this humble attitude when it comes to angels like us. I enjoy my work. I enjoy serving the living King, Jesus Christ, and I enjoy doing the works of the kingdom. Even when Matthew isn't sending us out or ministering, we temper the anointing in his life and we adjust the anointing day in and day out, depending on what sort of anointing he needs for the day. We haven't come to his attention very often; he is able to live with angels in his life without actively thinking about them all the time. We've all got our jobs to do in Matthew's ministry and Matthew's life, and we just get on and do our job.

It's a misconception to think that humans have to command angels. Every angel in the universe gets their permissions and authority from God. We're quite busy doing what we're told to do. We don't necessarily need human charges to order us around. There are a lot of people speaking about commanding angels, and there are a lot of people preaching about it, making reputations for themselves. I just like to say that we're quite capable.

Another thing that you might consider is that God's angels have never sinned—only Satan's angels have sinned. So, the idea of a sinful person commanding us is something that should give you pause. You'd have to be very well directed by the Spirit of the Lord and have good practice in being led by the Holy Spirit to dare to presume that you could send us out on a mission.

I hope that you can feel the weight of what I'm saying—that it's not just something that a person who sits on a pew each weekend does. Only people who serve the Lord and who are active have the opportunity to command angels. I want to encourage you that if you pursue Jesus, if you go after Jesus and get a reputation for obeying Him, there's a good chance that Jesus will allow angels to manifest in your life, and you can have a say in the affairs of God through using the angelic.

Matthew knows his ability and he knows what he can do, and yet he rarely calls on me. He just simply feels the effect of the presence of the angels and rarely tells me to do anything. That's not because it's wasted. I'm busy doing things myself, and my angels are busy ministering in Matthew's ministry. I hope that gave you some enlightenment and understanding into what's going on.

Meeting Mark—A Finance Angel

My next subject is Mark's effect in my life. As a person who has spent $130,000 AUD on self-publishing 59 books, I have a great need for income. Years ago, I was reading a book on angels by a person who had a series of three books on angels. I read in the first book that there are such things as finance angels. When I read that chapter, I asked the Lord if I had a finance angel, and the Lord said, "You have now!" I looked across the room and there was an angel there, and I asked him, "What's your name?" He answered, "My name is Mark."

I was able to remember the name Mark because, many years ago, a friend of mine at the time had a guy that she felt God had said was going to be her husband. The guy had blocked her on Facebook, wasn't taking phone calls or texts and had made it very clear that he wasn't interested in her. But she was determined that God had given her prophecies that he was going to be her husband. His name was Mark, so it was easy to remember that name because of this pseudo-love affair that this woman had.

In the book on angels, the author said that if you have a financial need, you can tell your financial angel to go and get that need. I needed $350 to publish the next book, so I took that instruction. I didn't have a prophetic website at the time that generated finances for me, so I said to Mark, "Can you go and get that finance for me in the next week?" Within the next week, $450 was given to me. One person gave me $200, one person gave me $100, and I got a check for $150 from the United Kingdom for royalties on my book that used to come every six months. So, I got $450 when I asked for $350. I realized that these financial angels really work!

I don't know about you, but I've got low self-esteem when it comes to things of God, and that means I don't often ask God for anything. I have an issue with asking for things. Most of the time when I ask for things, I'm asking for someone else. I'm praying for someone else. I don't often ask for things for myself. From time to time, people ask me what I need and I have trouble finding something to give them to pray for.

So, I said to Mark, "I have a problem asking for things. Can you do me a favor as a finance angel? Can you supply the finances that I need for my ministry to publish books?" For three and a half years, I published one book a month. So, I published 45 books in three and a half years, and I chewed up $2,000 AUD (about $1,400 USD) a month in publishing costs. I had a really good editor at the time who was expensive.

Mark put it on the hearts of people to request prophecies and prophetic services from my ministry website. He also put it on people's hearts just to give me money—40% of my ministry income has been from people's donations supporting me. It's just Mark's influence in people's lives. He speaks to people like the

Holy Spirit would speak to a person. He may say to them, "Give Matthew $1,000" or "Give Matthew $200" or "Give Matthew $20." Mark ministers for me, and he's always in ministry. There's only been a couple of times when I had to wait a couple of days for finances, but most of the time he's been ministering for me and raising finances.

Many people would hear this and say to themselves that they could do with a finance angel. But for what? What are you spending your finances on? Are you spending it on Armani suits and Prada handbags? Or Nike T-shirts and shoes? Are you going after all the lust of the world? Or are you in ministry? If you're in ministry and you need finances for ministry, isn't God already looking after you? If you need God to look after you and you're in ministry, it's quite okay to ask for a finance angel. Simply ask God for a finance angel, feel the presence of the angel, ask God what his name is and ask him to supply your finances.

Mark has been financing my ministry for almost five years. He's never missed a payment, and only twice have I had to wait. One time I had to wait for about a week. Though I will say that my book sales have been way down over the last year for some reason, and my income from them has halved. Now I'm not using my expensive editor. I'm using a cheaper editor, and so the quality of my books is less than that of the perfect books I used to produce. I think also that heaven wanted that. The editor now is 10% of the price of the one I used to pay for, and that used to chew up 70% of the money I spent on a book I was publishing. So, even though my ministry income has been halved, because I'm using the cheaper editor now, I've always got finances for the things I need.

You may be interested in hearing from a finance angel. I'd be interested in hearing what Mark has to say too. This is an angel that's been working in my life for four to five years and doing a wonderful job. I'll just put Mark on and see what he has to say.

Mark speaks

Hi, my name is Mark, and it's a real joy to minister for Matthew and work on his ministry. If it sounds strange that I'm a finance angel and I supply finances for Matthew, just think of it like being a marketing consultant for a business. A marketing consultant arranges all the marketing for the business, puts out the promotions and the sales, manages the website and does everything to do with marketing for business. I'm just like a marketing consultant for Matthew. I promote his books, I promote Matthew as a person, and I promote his ministry. Many people don't understand how angels talk. Many people have got no idea how often their guardian angel talks to them. They've got no idea how we can slide thoughts into a person's mind and then continue to slide thoughts in until they make a decision.

I don't go and harass people. Matthew hasn't got a mailing list. He's one of the few ministries that's got either 1,000 or 2,000 email addresses, but he never emails people. Matthew doesn't believe in professional mailing lists and professional marketing. He believes all of that is of the world. If you're getting a daily or weekly email from a ministry through the programs that you're subscribed to, it's normally annoying junk mail and they're always trying to sell you things. Mathew is never going to do that in ministry. He's got me. All I do is when people read his books and he puts the appeals in for finances at the end of his books, I move on people. I try to move on everyone like the Holy Spirit moves on people. I suggest to people, "Hey, give Matthew some finances", but not everyone's obedient to my thoughts.

I may lead them to read another book. When they read that part at the end, I may move on them again, like the Holy Spirit will move on you, and suggest, "Hey, donate some money to Matthew." Some people, rather than just giving, may choose to order a service from Matthew as a way of giving to him. Some people might want to purchase a personal prophecy. Some people may want an angel message. Some people may want a prophetic blueprint from Matthew.

As long as I'm leading him to a person who gets one of these prophetic services, they all earn Matthew money. But Matthew most likes people to just donate money, so he doesn't have to spend his time doing a prophetic service. So, I work similarly to the Holy Spirit in speaking to people. It's a funny thing, speaking to people about subjects like this, because people are so lacking in their understanding. Very few people understand how the Holy Spirit works. Very few people can actually hear the Holy Spirit or have a conversation with the Holy Spirit. The Holy Spirit's a bit of a mystery to most people.

It's mysterious how the Holy Spirit even directs or promotes things or does things with Christians, let alone talking about how an angel does it. So, if you understood how the Holy Spirit influences and leads people, then you'd understand a little bit more about how I do it—it's very similar to the Holy Spirit. I don't possess a person; I don't come into a person's house and bug them and bug them and bug them until they give Matthew money. I just move on their heart and say something like, "Gee, that was a really good book. That really touched me!" And that's their own thoughts saying that. "Jesus, it's a really good book. It's really touched me. I'd love to support him to make more books like this. I think I'll support him." They'd get that thought, and they'd think it was their thought, but it was me speaking. It's like me speaking into their mind, "Gee, that's a good book. I'd love to support him. I'll support him next month. When I get that bonus from work, I'll send him $1,000." And then next month, when they get the bonus, they get a thought, "I'd better find Matthew's website and support him like I said I would."

Now, it's not cheating that we do that. We speak in the resonance of your own thoughts; that's what Satan and his demons are doing all the time. You don't get temptations so much from your flesh, you get temptations from demons. But you think it's your own flesh doing that. A lot of men, for instance, look at girls and hope that they can get them naked and have sex with them. It is demons saying that to them, but they think it's their own thoughts. So, a lot of people haven't got an understanding of how thoughts work and how the angelic or the spiritual realm works. A lot of people, especially men, are walking around thinking they're such lustful people when it's actually a demon of lust that's speaking to them and making those suggestions in their head.

I work in people's minds and promote Matthew. I'm his promoter. If you're a person who follows Matthew or requested a prophecy from Matthew or written an email to Matthew, you can be sure that he's never written to you without you first contacting him. He's delivered the prophecy, or whatever service you have asked for, but that's the only time he's written to you.

Now, some of you have donated a sizable sum to Matthew, and he may have written an email back saying thanks. But that was the last email you got. You can reach out to Matthew, join him on Facebook and become a friend and start talking to him. You may write an email to him, and he may write an email to you when you are friends. But he doesn't do slick, clever, worldly marketing. He's got 2,000 or more email addresses of people who requested services, and he could write to all of them and do a slick campaign and sell something. But he doesn't. We do his marketing. The Bible says, *"Freely you have received, freely give,"* and Matthew does this because he gives these books away for 99 cents.

We can help people by saying to them, "Hey, this is a good sort of person, and this is the sort of ministry you want to support. You just got a wonderful book for 99 cents, and it's worth $10. Why don't you give him $50 for five of these books? Why don't you make up the five books for $10 each, give him $50 and say thanks for your books as a bonus?"

The sales of these books plus the money that comes through his website are earnings, and then the donations are separate, and he uses donation money as well as these earnings to produce books. One year he spent $45,000 on producing books, so he spends a lot of money.

So, if you want a finance angel to support your ministry, just put your hand up in the air now. I'll have Matthew pray for you. See you later. I hope this has been informative to you. I'll just have Matthew pray.

Matthew speaks

This is Matthew. If you're in ministry and you're honestly serving the Lord, and you're not squandering money on different things, I'll pray for you.

Dear Father, for everyone who's watching this video, for everyone who's reading this book who is honestly in ministry and needs help financially, I ask that you dispatch your finance angel to their ministry right now. I see them arriving in ministries, and I see the future. Help them understand that all they need to do is ask the Holy Spirit or ask you for the name of their finance angel, and the finance angel will be dispatched to meet their finance needs. I pray all this in Jesus's name. Amen.

So, we've talked about Jonathan and we've talked about Mark. These are both angels that I have effective, ongoing and lasting ministries with. Now we're going to talk about Bethany. Bethany is my scribe angel.

Bethany's effect in my life

I'll talk about what she does in my life, and then we'll hear from her. I'd love to show you pictures of all the angels. Bethany looks like the actress Keira Knightley; you can check her out on the Internet. You'll find that Bethany looks very pretty. Bethany is a scribe angel. In other words, she's like the Holy Spirit when it comes to my Facebook posts, videos, and books. Even though I'm speaking here in this video and it's coming through my intellect, the source of my words isn't just my intellect—it's Bethany. Bethany not only helps me write my books by inspiring the words for me to say in my videos that become books, but she also helps me in the editing of those books.

She definitely not only inspires the books but also works with Mark to get the finances. She gives me ideas for covers and titles of books, like *How I Minister With Angels*, and that's what this book is about. It's not about angels—it's about how I effectively minister with angels and their effect in my life.

Bethany is involved in everything to do with my books. She helps me pick the picture for the cover of the book, she helps me with the title of the book, and she helps me get the chapter titles. She helps me in so many ways. She really is dearly loved. I don't often talk to her, but she knows that I love her. It's especially good to have a female angel. Much to the dismay of some theologians, there is a reference in the Bible (which I'm not going to include here) to a stork, which is a female angel. Many Christians don't think female angels exist. Females exist in all the animals, and females exist in the human race, yet apparently females can't exist in the angelic! Well, they do exist, and Bethany is beautiful. So, Bethany inspires the books, and she gets the ideas for the books.

Actually, interestingly enough, it wasn't Bethany who inspired this book. It was a witch that I saved and led to the Lord, and who is with me at the moment. She inspired me to do this book today because she's with me right now. But Bethany gave me the book title and the chapter titles. Bethany's working with me and speaking through me; she's very much involved in this book. I've produced 59 books, and Bethany's been around for 50 of those. So, she's done a lot of work! There's a lot of reward in heaven for Bethany for the work she's done.

Here's another thing. Mark isn't playing, or twiddling his thumbs, and he's not sitting around doing just anything. Every day when finance comes into my ministry, Mark's been involved. Bethany is not just sitting around twiddling her thumbs, either. Every day I post on Facebook, every day I make a video, Bethany's involved. So she's busy.

I think it'd be interesting for you, especially women, to hear from a female angel. I'll let Bethany speak now.

Bethany, a scribe angel, speaks

Hi, this is Bethany. It's wonderful to meet all you women out there. Go, girl power! I'm a woman and I am a woman angel and I love what I look like. Matthew loves Keira Knightley as an actress. Interestingly enough, we led him to a few Keira Knightley films so that he came to love and follow her. Then one day, we were talking back and forth as he was walking down to a station in the city. I said to him, "Do you want to know what I look like?" This was before he used to do guardian angel messages, so he wasn't able to be led by the Holy Spirit to see what people's angels look like. He said, "Yeah, who do you look like?" I said, "I look like Keira Knightley." He went home to his computer and put Keira Knightley on his laptop dashboard and looked at her, then looked at me.

For a number of years, I've really enjoyed ministering to Matthew. I've been the author of other books in times past, but I'm not going to mention them (and I'm certainly not going to mention one of them, because you'd never believe it!). But I certainly don't work with any other authors now—I only work with Matthew. He puts enough books out to keep me busy! Like he said, I inspire many of his Facebook posts and a lot of his videos. I also inspire his books or write the titles of various chapter headings. So I do a lot.

Matthew's theology, his doctrine, is very much aligned with heaven. It's easy to work with Matthew. He's productive, busy, good to work with, he's learned how to minister out of rest, and he's able to have good rest and relaxation. He's able to be led really easily by the Holy Spirit, and he's able to be led by us. Even today, he was inspired to do this by a witch. She doesn't like being called a witch now because she's a Christian, but she's a former witch and she's really impressed with this book.

I'm here to tell you that if you're a writer, and you're going to make a business out of writing a number of books, then you could get a scribe angel. In fact, Joyce Meyer and other people who have written quite a number of books have scribe angels. Joyce has written a lot of books and she probably has no awareness that she's got a scribe angel. Actually, Matthew's heard that she's got people that ghostwrite for her, and Matthew assumes that could be true. But she's definitely got a scribe angel. We like to work with and be around people whose hands are busy. Angels also like to hang around people who have a relationship with the Lord and who want to serve the Lord. We don't like our time being wasted.

An hour before starting to write this book, Matthew had no idea that this book was going to come through. He didn't even know he had enough angelic stories to make a book. Yet the theme of this book isn't so much angelic stories. The theme is how to work and minister with angels, and also how to have a long-lasting and ongoing relationship with angels. Ministering with angels is effectively what Matthew has going on in his life.

It's great to talk to you. Whether you are watching the video or reading the book, if you're able to communicate with the Holy Spirit and you've got spiritual ears and you can hear things, look up a picture of Keira Knightley, then say hello to me and listen to me speak to you, voice-to-voice and mind-to-mind. Then ask me a question and see if I answer you. You can talk to me, and that would be fun. It's been good talking to you. I hope I've been informative. Just remember the key point I made: angels like to hang around busy people, people who are busy ministering for the Lord. Got to be busy, folks! Okay, I'll hand you back to Matthew. (Oh, and I have a sweet surprise for you. If you look at the cover of this book, you'll notice an image with a resemblance to me.)

Now this is Matthew speaking.

Meeting Michael—My Guardian Angel

Now we're going to talk about my guardian angel, who is called Michael. Michael has been my guardian angel ever since I was born. I was about 14 years of age when I had some healing done called "healing of the memories." It's like prophetic, spiritual healing where people ask you questions and take you back to a certain time. They have Jesus talk to you to heal the memory, and then this heals you. I went to bed and I couldn't get to sleep. That had never happened to me in my life before, as I was a good sleeper. An hour after going to bed, I went in and woke my mom up and I said, "I can't get to sleep!" I used to always wake my mother up when I was sick. She got up and gave me a sleeping pill. I went back to bed, stayed there an hour and a half, and woke my mom up again. She gave me a second sleeping pill. She said, "If you can't sleep now, don't wake me up. I've giving you more than a child should take. Just wait until the morning and read a book or do something." I went back to bed and I was there for about 40 minutes—dead awake. I couldn't go to sleep. The sleeping pill was having no effect.

I had a good relationship with Jesus. I've been a Christian since I was eight years old and had a two-way conversational relationship with Jesus. So, I asked Jesus what my angel's name was. He said, "Your angel's name is Michael." I put my hand in the air. I said, "Michael, hold my hand." Electricity went through my hand as soon as I said that. That's the last thing I remember, and then I woke up in the morning. That was my first encounter with Michael. I found out Michael's name by asking Jesus what my angel's name was, and that was the key.

Here's another key for you: if you want to work with angels, and if you want to have a relationship with them, go through Jesus. Jesus has always got the answers. If you want to know your angel's name and he won't tell you—ask Jesus. If Jesus won't tell you the name, He'll tell you the reason why.

I've got a service on my website where you can write to me and I'll tell you the name of your guardian angel. I'll send you a picture that looks like your guardian angel, and I'll give you a five-minute message from the guardian angel. Jesus has released me to do that. There hasn't been anyone who has requested one and the Holy Spirit said, "No, don't do this."

Michael's been with me all of my life. About eight years ago, he got a promotion to become my prophetic angel. I used to minister in the prophetic. I've been ministering in the prophetic, talking to strangers and doing prophetic evangelism for 20 years. For people who don't know, prophetic evangelism is giving a prophetic message to a stranger by just walking up to them and giving them a message from God. That's really effective in Australia, because 95% of Australians don't go to church, which is different than America. Normally, when I've done prophetic evangelism, I'll be shown a person by the Holy Spirit. The Holy Spirit will tell me something about a person's character or life.

When I get that message from the Holy Spirit, I'll approach the person and tell them. That's normally the way I do things.

There have been certain times in my life when I could tell something about everyone in the supermarket. It wasn't just one here, one there—it was everyone. I noticed this and it was amazing. I've since found out that's walking in the glory. When you've got the glory on you, that's what you can do—you can have a prophetic message for anyone. Most of these people are non-Christians, so it's not just ministering to 100 Christians in the church. God's got a message for everyone, even atheists and witches.

When I first got this anointing, I didn't know what it was. I just thought it was an anointing, but in fact it's the glory realm. I used to call this anointing, this ability to know something about everyone in a shopping center, "the 100% anointing." It would come upon me and I could get a message for everyone. When Michael got promoted and became a prophetic angel and I found out, I asked him whether he could bring that 100% anointing, as I used to call it. If you read my book, *Prophetic Evangelism Made Simple*, you'll notice I used to call it "100% anointing" because I didn't know what glory was, and I had no grid for what glory was.

Most people who are ministering the glory can explain it very well, but I used to call it 100% anointing. When I asked Michael to give me the 100% anointing, he would do something which put glory on me. It's pretty easy for him. But he could put me into the 100% anointing, and then I could have sport and just walk up to 20 people in an hour and give them prophecies.

Michael ministers through the use of my prophetic gift, just like Bethany speaks through me and ministers through my books and videos and my Facebook posts. Michael's speaking according to the Holy Spirit, of course, because every angel is led by the Holy Spirit. He's been really effective and really good for my life. However, we don't talk a lot. It's interesting that we've talked about Jonathan, Mark, Bethany and now Michael, but I don't talk very often with any of them or have conversations with them every day. They're there and they do their job. It's like part of your team in a workplace. If you had 100 staff, you wouldn't be talking to each one of your 100 staff every day. For example, you might have a marketing director who looks after all of your marketing projects. If she needs to have a meeting with you because there's a major decision that needs to be made, then maybe you'll talk to her in that meeting. But then she'll go off and do her job. Your assistant will talk to her.

I want to explain this. Even if you've got a lot of angels ministering in your life, you're not necessarily communicating with them all the time. It doesn't mean they're not effective, and it definitely doesn't mean that they're not doing their job. This means I'm not fascinated by angels. Actually, that's probably why I've got a lot of them in my life—because I don't bow down to them. I don't worship them and I'm not fascinated by them. If you want to find a person who mixes with a lot of angels, check out the author Michael Van Vlymen. He's got a number of books on angelic encounters, and I'm sure you'll find them fascinating.

It's good to find a Christian who talks about angels instead of New Age people. I don't discount that New Age people have met angels just because they're not Christians, but you can't really trust everything that's said in those books.

So, Michael my guardian angel has been with me since I was young, and I've known of him since my school days. I've definitely used 100% anointing from time to time. I'll have Michael speak to you now.

Michael the guardian angel speaks

This is Michael. I want to tell you that you can have an angel in your life for so many different things. You've even got an angel who can lead you to a specific book on Amazon. Yesterday, for instance, Matthew searched for "end times" on Amazon, and he found a book called *As in the Days of Noah.* He went to the book page and read the reviews and found that it was written by a certain author. He went to the author's home page and looked at his other books. He was attracted to another book from the author on the topic of apostasy. He decided to download that Audible book and now he's listening to that. How did he get to the book on apostasy? I told him to search for "end times." He searched for "end times," he saw *As in the Days of Noah*, and he clicked on it because I told him to. Then he looked at the other books by the author because I told him to. He got to that author's page that listed all his books, and he's now listening to the book I led him to, and it's a great book on apostasy. I have shown him that a co-writer of that book has a book on finances and heavenly rewards. He's going to read that book, too!

If you understand the process that we took Matthew through to find the book on apostasy, you will find that, instead of a person's intuition leading them, it is the voice of their guardian angel inspiring their decisions and thoughts. Actually, Mark possibly led you to Amazon to find this book. If you think about it, it would be difficult to find this book using the search term 'angels' because there are so many books on the subject of angels. When you understand the ministry of guardian angels, you'll be shocked at what we get up to, besides just protecting people from accidents.

Getting back to the story, Matthew has another credit on Audible, so he can buy that book on heavenly rewards. Matthew is very much into heavenly rewards, and so should you be. But very many Christians out there spend all their money on the things of the Earth with no eternal reward. That's just how people are.

An angel can lead you through Amazon to a specific book, and that's what a guardian angel does all the time. As you look at the side of your YouTube channel, your guardian angel can pick another video and they will lead you from that one to another one to another one. They can get you watching something God wants you to watch. A guardian angel can tell you, "You should ring your mother," and then repeat it when you don't ring her— "You should ring your mother, you should ring your mother!"

The guardian angel can also encourage you in the Lord and encourage you to grow in intimacy with Jesus. Honestly, if you want to learn about guardian angels, go and read the book called *A Message from my Angel*, which includes 30 five-minute messages from guardian angels. Or if you don't want to spend 99 cents, go and listen to Matthew's YouTube playlist of messages from guardian angels. If you listen to the YouTube playlist, you can actually hear them speaking through him, and they're all minimum five-minute messages.

If you listen to 100 messages on YouTube, you will see they all have a different message and a different personality. You'll find guardian angels do a tremendous number of things in people's lives—they're amazing! People have no understanding of what we can do as guardian angels. So much of Matthew's life is directed. He hardly makes any choices or does anything he wants to do because nearly everything he does is what we direct him to do, and because of that, he's now free of major sins in his life. Nearly everything he does in his life is directed by the Holy Spirit or by me, and nearly everything he says is Bethany or the Holy Spirit speaking, or an angel or someone else speaking.

I encourage you, if you're reading this book, to go to Matthew's website and get your own angel message from him. Then you'll know the name of your angel, and you'll see a picture of your angel. If the picture is familiar, it's meant to be familiar. You'll also get a five-minute message from your angel. If you have a picture of your angel, a message from your angel and your angel's name as a starting point, at least there's a chance that you might be able to start communicating with your angel.

I'm not here selling Matthew's service to you, but he does like doing the angel messages because he gets to meet the person's guardian angel every time he does one. Over the course of the last four years, he's met hundreds of guardian angels. He loves doing those messages. If you're watching this, or reading this book, go to his YouTube playlist on guardian angel messages and listen to a few. If you've listened to a few and you liked them, order one for yourself. I'll pass you back to Matthew now.

The effect of Michael the Archangel on my life

Over the course of the last 20-25 years, I've met Michael the Archangel about 50 times. Many times, I have been under stress and Michael has turned up to protect me or speak for me.

One time I remember may sound quite violent to you. A young prophet was disagreeing with me. Michael turned up, stood next to me for a time and then stepped into me. He said to this young prophet, "This is an angel speaking through Matthew now. Now, repeat what you said. Tell Matthew that he doesn't know what he's saying, and he doesn't know the truth of the matter. Say that Matthew's lying and he's not telling the truth. If you say that, something's going to hit you in the stomach. It's going to come out of Matthew's belly. Matthew's hand isn't going to move, but something's going to hit you in the stomach and you're going to land 100 feet away. So just say Matthew doesn't know what he's saying."

The young prophet went white, which suggested he didn't have anything to say. "So, Matthew's wrong? Is Matthew wrong, or have you got nothing to say? If you have nothing to say, then walk away and don't ever approach Matthew again. If Matthew approaches you, you can talk to him, but don't you ever approach him again." And he walked away. Then I went upstairs; Michael was with me and he had about 2,000 angel generals with him. These are archangels that are first in line for Michael's commands.

My friend Yianni asked me, "Matthew, why do you always have to do things like that?"

I said, "Well, I didn't do it. Michael did it, and here are 2,000 of his generals. Can you see all these guys?"

My friend agreed that he could see them. I asked him how many angels there were in the city and Yianni said the whole city was full of angels. Yianni was convinced by the angelic visit that the altercation was authentic, but he didn't like it. You may also not like that story, and I only leave it in the book to show you that Michael loves me and protects me, and sometimes will show up and make his presence felt. I have had other occasions when angels have shown up and people have frozen and gone white.

Michael the Archangel speaks

Matthew financed an important book for an important prophet in 2017-18. The Holy Spirit told him to send $1,000 USD to the prophet to help him self-publish his book. Then the angel over Australia and myself came into his life. He was a little bit freaked out as to why we were in his life and wouldn't leave his house. He asked his counselor at the time what we were there for, and his counselor said to him that he needed protection at this time. For nine months, we were in his house, and thousands of witches astral travelled into his house at that time. He really did need protection. Matthew was led to believe that he had started a revival for witches, but they were fooling him.

The witches almost had him killed a couple of times, so we really needed to protect him. People would say I couldn't be at Matthew's house, but I can bilocate and be in two places at once. People say I'm the angel of Israel, which means I'm always in Israel, so I can't come to Australia. People assume a lot of things, especially about things of God. Unless they're God, unless they're really hearing from God, they make a lot of wrong assumptions. I'm a personal friend of Matthew's and I've come to his rescue a number of times. I've ministered with Matthew.

Jonathan's just one of my angels. He's not even an archangel. Jonathan's just a lower-level angel in charge of 6 million angels.

You'll hear of an angel later in this book called Gamiel. Gamiel is one of my frontline archangels. He is currently in Matthew's life and he won't be leaving. He's a new angel. All the guardian angels and fighting angels are under my command. You may get to know me and meet me. When you're totally sold out to Jesus, when you're one of the best servants of Jesus on Earth, then you'll get to know me. Apart from that, what would be the use of meeting me? I've got billions of angels under my command. Why would I need to come into you? I'm not saying that in a prideful way through Matthew, I'm just saying. Not all the accounts of people meeting Michael the Archangel are real.

One time, Matthew was driving a taxi and he was waiting at a university stop at Queensland University, a place where taxis line up. A businessman, who was me in disguise, walked up to him. The man got in the front seat and put his briefcase in the backseat. Matthew said, "How was your day? Did you get much done today?"

"Yes, I had a good day today", I replied.

Matthew asked, "What did you get up to?"

I said, "We're not going to talk about me today. We're going to talk about you. How's your life going?"

Matthew replied, "Pretty good."

I said, "Well, I'm going to ask you again, how's your life been going?"

Soon enough, Matthew was talking and crying, in tears about going through a custody battle and divorce. I was able to counsel him and show him from scripture that you're not meant to take a Christian to court and you're not meant to fight with your wife. I showed scripture after scripture, and I showed him why a custody battle and fighting over access to his son wasn't of God, and that he needed to drop all that and do what his wife wanted. I got out at the airport and he pulled off and went to drive away. Then he pulled the car back and ran in to find me, because he swore that I was an angel.

But I had disappeared and had gone back to heaven by then. He couldn't find me, though he searched the whole airport, and he knew I was an angel. He asked Jesus years later who that angel was. Jesus said that it was me. Matthew couldn't believe it. He asked why Jesus would send Michael the Archangel when any angel would have done.

Jesus said to Matthew that he was one of His best servants on Earth, and also one of His closest friends. Jesus said He sent me because the job had to be done and I wanted to do it. I wanted to meet Matthew in the flesh.

Since I know a little bit about heaven, I'll tell you something that may be of interest to you. When people pray, there's a big filing system in heaven, and all the prayers go in under people's names. They have years and years and years of files, and there is a certain day when each of the prayers will be answered. So, a person has all those prayers and they get put in a file, and every day, the prayers to be answered that day are pulled out from the files. As you can imagine, billions of prayers get pulled out every day. Of course, one day of Earth time is about three weeks of heaven time, but it's still a daily thing in heaven.

Now, one of your prayers may be that your husband goes to another level in his relationship with Jesus. You've been praying that prayer for 10 years, but on that particular day it comes out of the prayer file and is given to me along with millions of other prayers. I dispatch that work to all my archangel generals. Let's say you're an American, because most people reading Matthew's books are American, and you're in Chicago. The prayer request is sent to the Angel of America, and the Angel of America dispatches it to the State Angel of Illinois, and then the State Angel gives it to the City Angel of Chicago; then the Chicago angel dispatches it to an angel in the suburbs of the city. That angel says to a friend of your husband's, "Give your friend (your husband) this book, *Angels on Assignment*, today as he's leaving his house."

He sees the book and gives it to the husband as a gift, saying, "Hey, I just read this book called *How I Minister with Angels* by Matthew Robert Payne and it was a really good book. It mentioned this book, *Angels on Assignment*, and said it was really good. I remembered I had it. I haven't read it for years, but I thought I'd give it to you. You have to read it."

So, you've been praying for 10 years, and one day your request comes all the way to that friend of your husband. Your husband starts reading it and he gets fired up. Then he finds and reads this book and discovers that he is mentioned in it. He'll say to himself, "Well, I'm from Chicago and my wife's been praying this prayer and here I am reading this book that I'm mentioned in!"

That's how it happens! Prayers come out of the filing system in heaven and they're given to me. I dispatch them all to my frontline archangels, who dispatch every angel over every country. Every country has their own angel. For example, it says in the Bible that I am the angel over Israel, so all the work in Israel is dispatched by me. The angel of the country dispatches it and it goes out until it comes to the warring angel, guardian angel or any sort of angel who can get the job done. You can be sure that when the prayer came up that Matthew's mother was praying about a child custody case and she didn't want him to go to court, that prayer came out for the day. When it came through, I said, "I'll do that!" So, I went to work as a human and delivered that message. It was very impactful for Matthew. He dropped the custody case and that changed his life.

Angels can have an effect on people's lives. You can be sure your prayers can be answered by angels. But remember that some prayers don't get put into the filing system in the first place. Some prayers don't align to the will of God, and so they get missed.

You've got prayers in that filing system. There are women, young women and middle-aged women, praying for their husbands. The answers to these prayers are in that filing system, and there are answers. Psalm 37:4 says, *"Delight yourself in the Lord and He will give you the desires of your heart."* Also, if you're waiting for a husband, take time and delight yourself in the Lord and He'll give you the desires of your heart. That's the verse you should concentrate on.

I've been used in Matthew's life. For a year I was in his house and protecting him. He had a lot of activity happening in the house for a year. He'll cover that in a book he's going to do about his experiences with witchcraft.

What else do you want to hear from me? One of you in the future, when you're reading the book, pop out a question and I'll answer it. One person reading the book asked, "Are you really a good fighter?" I am a fighter, and I'm a really good fighter. I have generals that fight at the front, but I've got a lot of fighting angels that are really experienced. Here's something you may not know. Archangels are like four stories high, but when they're inside a building they are six foot seven. Inside, we are imposing in height and very muscular, but outside we can be four stories tall. Matthew has an angel called Gamiel in his life who is a four-story angel. He walks with Matthew outside and people can see a four-story angel beside him.

One of you asked about your prayers and how you can increase their effectiveness. Jesus taught that if you continue in your prayers, He'll do what you ask. Another thing that will affect your prayers is to make sure you're not lusting after things. God's not going to answer your prayers for a finance angel for more finances if you're lusting after the things of the world. God's not going to answer prayers like that. He's going to answer your prayers according to John 15—if you abide in Jesus and are obeying Jesus's commands and teachings. If you're not abiding in Jesus, your prayers won't be answered as often.

There's different varying effects. Many people say, "Well, if you pray according to God's will, it'll happen." Yeah, that's right. But how do you know God's will? This is a very complex question. That's why there are so many books about prayer. But until you've learned to walk in the Holy Spirit, and be directed by the Holy Spirit, you're probably not going to be directed in prayer. That's why praying in tongues is such a good option because you pray the things you're meant to be praying. If you're not Pentecostal or charismatic and you don't believe in tongues, then you're always going to struggle with what to pray unless you can be led by the Holy Spirit. The Holy Spirit can pray a prayer similar to tongues. When Matthew prays a prayer for someone else, it's like he's speaking in tongues in English, which Paul mentioned—it's prayer with understanding, which is tongues in English.

Paul didn't pray flesh prayers. Paul prayed prayers led by the Holy Spirit, and every word was directed by the Holy Spirit, but it was in his natural tongue. You can learn to pray prayers like that which are very effective prayers. But you have to be walking really close to the Holy Spirit to be able to pray like that. Matthew learned to pray like that and so can you.

One more answer to a question. Yes, I'm going to vanquish Satan in the future. But Satan's like a dog on a leash. He still takes commands from Jesus and from God. He still has to do what we tell him to do, even though he hates us. Even though he fought against us, he still takes orders from us. So many people involved in warfare bring warfare on themselves for trying to attack Satan. I'll just leave it with you that the people who seem to think they know most about warfare actually cause a lot of people trouble. I'm going to go and hand you back to Matthew.

Let's talk about Gamiel the Archangel

This is Matthew speaking. We're now going to talk about Gamiel, who is the new archangel that's come into my life and had an effect in my life. Once again, Gamiel was prophesied by Auty. About three months ago, he did a prophecy and said there would be a new angel coming into my life, an archangel. I thought it was amazing that an archangel would come into my life because that's one of the highest forms of angels. It turns out he's one of Michael's most trusted guys. Gamiel can command a lot of angels, not just 6 million. He's an archangel, and he's four stories high.

Both the Angel of Australia and Michael are four stories high too when they're outside, and when they want to be. Of course, that can be very intimidating. They can walk beside you and be hidden so no one can see them. They can appear four stories high to people or they can appear as six foot seven, depending on what they want to be. It's really up to heaven how they appear. It's not up to you if you've got a four-story angel with you, and it's not up to you to decide how that angel manifests, or whether it manifests at all.

So, Gamiel is his name, and he has brought a measure of glory into my life. Glory is a level of the manifested presence of God. Glory makes your skin shine and makes little kids look at you. Glory makes people who need direction come to see you. Glory allows strangers to listen to you more when you approach them and start talking to them; they're more receptive and will give you more time to talk to them. Glory brings things to you and has favor on them. Glory has a whole lot of effects on people and on your life.

Also, glory gets the attention of witchcraft. When witches and warlocks see and feel the glory they will sometimes attack you. I'll share more about witchcraft in an upcoming book, but I'll share some things about the effect of glory on witchcraft in the last chapter of this book. There was a witch I met in a shop and the bank card reader wouldn't work. I tried it a couple of times; then she got frustrated and she used it and it worked. It was like a power play happening. She was wearing a pentagram, so I knew she was a witch.

I went outside and got something to eat, but she astral travelled out to me and started getting in my face. Gamiel marched into the shop and told her not to harass me and to leave me alone. Then I went shopping. As I was coming out of the shop twenty minutes later, she came to harass me again. Gamiel marched back into the shop and put the sword in her head and gave her a migraine. I went to have coffee and a cake to treat myself and she come through astral travel to get in my face. She said, "I don't care about the migraine, I'm going to get you." I said, "Oh, it's all right. Do what you like. I'm talking to this guy." I was talking to a guy about golf and having a good time listening to him. I basically just ignored her, which is really frustrating to a witch. I started talking to this guy and then I forgot about her.

When I got up to leave the shop, she said, "I can see you and I know you're going now. I'm going to follow you." I asked Gamiel in fear, "Is she following me?"

He said, "No, but she's got a hunt on. There are multiple witches and warlocks who are watching you now and astral traveling to see where you live."

I said, "So what's going on?" It's handy if you can talk to an angel who's protecting you.

Gamiel said, "You're going to walk to the end of the street and disappear—the witches won't be able to see you. Remember in scripture when Jesus disappeared among the crowd? Well, these are witches who are astral traveling. It's like they're there in the flesh and watching you. You're going to walk to the end of the street and disappear. The glory is going to take you, and angels are going to hide you."

So, I walked to that street and I disappeared, and it was all over. Well, about four days later, she appeared again when I was out, and she started getting in my face. Gamiel put a sword in her side, and she had an excruciating pain in her side similar to having her appendix burst. She was given a thought by Gamiel that said, "You've not only got the migraine now, but you've got this excruciating pain. It's going to last for two hours. When the two hours is finished, it's going to stop. Don't you ever approach Matthew without our permission again or you'll get that pain again."

You may question an angel giving a person a migraine or an excruciating pain in the side, but this witch wanted to do more than argue with me.

Now Gamiel is going to talk to you.

Gamiel speaks

It's good to talk to you. Not many of you listening to this video or reading this book will ever have an archangel working with you or protecting you. Not many of you will move into the glory realm that Matthew moves in, and not many of you will really need someone like me, a fighting angel or a guardian angel, who can protect you from people and witches. Witches don't necessarily pick on the average Christian because they haven't got enough power, and they're not radiating enough power. Matthew can walk in the glory and we can strip the glory off him also. So, we can strip his power, or we can leave it on him. His encounters with witches have redemptive purposes.

I want you to know that our job is to serve and to help humans. I've got multiple purposes. Matthew hasn't had many conversations with me, but I've got multiple purposes in his life. I'm here for a reason, and not just protecting him from witches, which is a pretty low-level task. Not many people need a four-story angel to travel with them just to protect them from a witch here and there. But Matthew and I haven't gotten into why I'm here.

Once again, I'll remind you that Matthew has a number of angels in his life who are always there. He hasn't bothered to ask us, and doesn't even feel inspired to ask us what we're here for and what we're doing. There's a popular message Matthew's heard a couple of times from a couple of speakers: angels are sitting around bored, so you've got to get them to work and give them commands in order to keep them busy. That's just heresy. We know what to do and we get our commands from God. We don't need humans to tell us what to do. That's heresy, and I need to be bold and tell you that. I don't care who's saying it. It's ego and heresy.

We're pretty powerful. We're anointed, and we move in the glory realms. Matthew has talked about glory, and now I am talking about glory realms. There are different levels of anointing that you can get promoted to, and Matthew got promoted in his anointing 14 times in 2019; then he reached the first stage of glory. You start in glory realms. To help explain, I'll tell you a little story about the glory. Matthew used to take people on visits to heaven, and he's going to offer that from his website within the next week. By the time this book is published, you'll be able to book a trip to heaven with Matthew. Matthew used to do this years ago through his website.

However, when you experience heaven, there's a really strong level of the presence of God which is powerful. It's either really peaceful or joyful. The presence of God is not really a presence, and not anointing, but it is the glory realm. Sometimes the presence of God will come into a church, but it's blissful. Well, when Matthew took people to heaven, it was fine. They saw and experienced heaven and they enjoyed themselves. But it was like a hangover for Matthew when he came back. It was like he entered into a depression because he didn't want to come back from heaven. He loves heaven so much, and life has been so tough for him that he just didn't want to come back to Earth. So, he felt he was hurting himself through taking people to heaven because it was jolting his system. Experiencing the glory of heaven and then coming back to Earth was just too much for him.

Recently in the last couple of weeks, he's taken a couple of people to heaven and there hasn't been that jolt because Matthew is living in glory now. He is in the glory realm and he's always got that joy and peace. It's no longer a jolt when he comes back. I bring that level of glory to his life and I keep the glory up. We can move it up and down depending on the day and on what we want to do.

There are a lot of mysteries. Just remember that people are key. You get to know mysteries when you're someone important. Mysteries aren't for novices. What's the use of finding out a mystery unless you're going to do something with it? There's a lot of mystery to angels and the angelic in the heavenly realms. I'd encourage you to seek God and seek intimacy with Jesus, which is the key to everything.

Commanding angels

This is Matthew speaking. We had bushfires in Australia at the beginning of 2020, especially from October-November 2019 to February-March 2020. My friend Auty wrote me an email one day and said, "You've got authority as a son of God to stop this fire. So, decree for the bushfires to stop." I did a decree and told angels to go out and stop the bushfires. The next day, two-thirds of the bushfires were put out by rain. So, you can command angels.

I also commanded angels to go and visit all the people in the sex industry in America in their dreams and lead them to Jesus and give them a salvation message. I put angels in their dreams about a friend or relative of theirs giving them the message of salvation and leading them to Jesus. I have also activated angels so that people have people they know approach them and lead them into Christianity and into a church. I put a whole campaign together that would last for six months, and I've had a lot of angels busy. Six million angels were put to work over the course of six months.

Commanding angels is a specific subject that I may write a book about. The first time the 2,000 commander angels turned up, I didn't know why they wouldn't leave. I asked the Holy Spirit what they were doing and why they didn't leave, and He told me they were waiting on a command from me. I asked someone online, and they suggested a person that has a popular reputation with angels. I listened to two 90-minute videos by this person that were supposed to be on the subject of commanding angels. The videos didn't teach me anything. I said so to the Holy Spirit, and the Holy Spirit said, "Why do people go to men? Why didn't you come to me? Now this is what you do—you have to work out how you're going to keep 6 million angels busy."

So, I sat down and worked out a flowchart: Get them to say this, then if they say yes, do this; if they say no, do this. If they say yes to that, do this; if they say no to that, do this. I worked out six months of work, which had a really good effect on the sex workers in the United States and all the victims of sexual abuse. You may know someone in that industry who was helped, but this was a couple of years ago so I can't really ask for testimony. But I did see something on the news that showed me that I'd had an effect.

One thing the Holy Spirit told me was that when I command angels, I should not look to the media to report the success of my mission. Why is that? Because Satan will use the lack of confirmation to make you think you're crazy, that you didn't do what you just did. The Holy Spirit warned me very clearly not to look for fruit; just do what you do by faith.

But I've seen confirmation with the bushfires. I've seen it with the Australian election, and I've seen it with Israel. I'll be led one day to do a book on commanding angels. I just want to collect a few stories to have a good book. I suppose I have so much effect commanding angels because I did some research that. But I didn't have to do much research on the Australian bushfires; I just made the decrees.

Guardian Angel messages

I have a service on my website at https://personal-prophecy-today.com where you can request a guardian angel message, as I shared before.

 You can request the name of your guardian angel, a message from the guardian angel, and a picture of your guardian angel. How do I get the picture? A name is given to me by the Holy Spirit, like Holly Jenkins, for example. Actually, I suspect there's a Holly Jenkins who's reading this book and I just said your name. But let's just say the name Holly Jenkins is given to me by the Holy Spirit. I type 'Holly Jenkins' into Google Images and I look through the pictures until the Holy Spirit impresses one of the pictures upon me. I pick the picture that stands out, which is illuminated by the Holy Spirit. Many times, the picture I choose looks a little like the person who requested a guardian angel message or like someone they recognize. It doesn't necessarily have to look like them. There is this popular theology that says your angel has to look like you. They say this because when the church was praying for Peter in the Bible an angel turned up, and they said it must be his angel. So, it's popular theology out there by many preachers who say your guardian angel has to look like you. Well, they can, but they don't have to. In any case, people can have more than one guardian angel.

I have done guardian angel messages for a friend. She requested six messages, and four of the pictures were spitting image of her friends. She wondered how I was getting pictures of her friends. The Holy Spirit just gives me a name. I look through all the pictures I find and pick one. I've been doing that for years, being led by the Holy Spirit, or probably by Bethany. I'm led by a name to search for a picture on a database of pictures.

To get a picture for one of my books, I type in a word and look through all the pictures until I find a picture that suits. I used to think that it was the Holy Spirit who would lead me to the right picture, but now I'm starting to think it was Bethany all the time. Unless you're led like me by Bethany or by the Holy Spirit, you couldn't simply type in 'Holly Jenkins' and find a picture that looks like that person's guardian angel. It's a real skill. It's a little skill and it's an easy skill, but most people can't do it.

I can get the name Susan Smith or Susan Phillips or maybe Jeremy Jenkins. Maybe two people with the last name Jenkins are reading this book. Whatever it is, I can find the picture.

The five-minute message from the angel is simple because you've seen in this book that I can dictate any voice. That's part of the prophetic, to be able to carry another voice. I can carry the voice of God, the voice of Jesus, the voice of an angel, the voice of a saint, the voice of my mother, the voice of my father, or the voice of Bob Jones. That's a prophetic gift—to be able to flow and hear and see. So, they're the guardian angel messages, and I challenge you to get one for yourself. They're $25 AUD, so about $18 USD. Order one for yourself and you'll be happy you did.

It is also a real skill to get angels' names for people, but once again it's a skill I could teach any prophetic person.

Satan's portal in my house

I had two portals in my house. For people who don't understand, a portal is like people in a worship band. They sing worship, and the worship breaks through heaven and brings heaven down to Earth. Well, instead of angels and saints and guardian visitors having to break through a whole lot of warfare, they can just enter through a portal in heaven and come directly into my kitchen. It's like going through a doorway in heaven and stepping out the other side into my house. For years, I've had angels and saints arrive in my house. My house has always been full of angels and I've always got people arriving.

What I didn't know is that Satan had two portals in my house too—one in the kitchen and one in my bedroom. The exact same portal had a portal next to it, which was Satan's. I used to wonder how a demon, how Satan and all sorts of ugly stuff used to get into my house. I was thinking, why don't the angels in and around my house protect me? Why am I always getting attacked? I could never solve it, and there really aren't many experts around. You may think there are a lot of experts in Christianity, but there aren't.

Auty has this service where he removes blockages and barriers to your faith. He did this new service for me because he thought people needed it. He did it for me for free. It was he that told me that Satan had two portals in my house. I said, "Well, I've definitely got to pay to get that fixed." He's $100 USD for an hour of his time. I paid for the blockages to be fixed, and that included the two portals of Satan. He took the portals out of my house and now nothing can get in my house.

They can only get in my house by my request, so the only way the witches can get in my house, if they ask me now, is if they're friendly. If they're not friendly, they can't get into my house. But for years Satan used to come through the portal. I couldn't understand. I thought there must be a portal that's open to the supernatural. That's what worked out. The supernatural can just get through these things. Yes, I've seen Satan come through.

So, a portal is just a place that they can come through, and now I haven't got demonic portals in my house. Things are a lot friendlier. It's good to have a house that's only got good people in it. I'm joking around with this. If you see this on video, you'll see me laughing, but it's actually pretty scary. One time I woke up with a man on my back. I told him to get off in Jesus's name and he went into my bedroom. I told him to go in Jesus's name, and he went into my living room. I told him to go from the living room and he went out the door. Then an hour later, he was on my back again, and someone was trying to rape me. It's not good having those things in your house. If you've got anything blocking you from breakthrough, and you believe you've got blockages or bondages in your life, then Auty is the man to see to get fixed up. He certainly fixed a whole lot of things for me. I'll put his contact info at the end of this book.

The Effect of Thousands of Angels Walking in the Glory

When you're walking in a good measure of glory, it will attract the attention of people who have power, which is normally witchcraft. As I promised, I'm going to finish this book with a story. It's about a witch I encountered a few weeks ago. A friend of my brother's is staying with me, and he took a camera my brother ordered and wanted to find out how to use it and get film for it. So, he went into a camera store in the city to ask for help. A lady there checked it out and said it needed repair at a certain shop. She gave us directions and we went walking to the shop to get the camera repaired. On the way to the shop, I passed a girl. She was looking down, but when she got to me, she looked up and looked me in the eye, and then kept on going.

I then met her down the road. She appeared next to me (by astral traveling). She said, "I know this is a Christian term—anointing. Where did you get your anointing from?" Because I can hear in the spirit, it was fine. I knew it was the girl from a minute ago. I knew she was asking questions, and now I knew she was a witch. A lot of Christians can't do this. Michael Van Vlymen can, and Auty probably can, but most Christians can't. I said, "The anointing came from a lot of patience, a lot of hard work, a lot of obedience and a great relationship with Jesus."

"How can I get that anointing?," she said.

I replied, "You first have to be a Christian."

She said, "How can I contact you?"

I said, "My name is Matthew Robert Payne, and you can contact me on social media."

She said, "How can I be your friend?"

"You can only be my friend if this angel with me agrees that you can be my friend. He's going to take you back to where you come from. You can talk to him," I replied.

Five minutes later, we were in the camera store. She turned up again. She said, "Your angel said I can be your friend."

I said, "Really?"

I said to Gamiel, "Gamiel, did you say she could be my friend?"

"Yes, she's friendly. She's okay, we're cool."

So, she came into my life and stayed with me the rest of the day. I asked her to travel with me and come to my house. The name of that witch who was saved in walking to the camera store was Katrina. She's here too and she wants to say something.

Katrina speaks

Hi, people! It's amazing that I turn up in a book, and I had no idea until my name was mentioned that Matthew was doing this. I just want to encourage you. If a friend of yours or someone you know is a witch, just put your arms around them and love them. That's all we need. You know, John Lennon and the Beatles had it right: "All you need is love." I've read a lot Matthew's books now, and I understand that if you distill the 50 commands of Jesus, the teachings of Jesus, you'll find that Jesus preaches the law of love. All the world needs is love.

There's too much religion. There's too much Christianity. There's not enough love. Learn to love people. Stop judging people and learn to love them. Accept people for who they are. Just love them; just love them. You will find if you accept people for who they are that they will open up to you. But they're not going to open up to someone that they feel judged by. The reason why your homosexual friends don't open up to you is because you don't accept them, and you don't love them. Matthew found in research that about 30% of witches are lesbians.

We've got two barriers—we're in darkness and we're lesbians. How are we going to be accepted by the church? All you need is love! Learn to love us. Just love us and accept us. God bless you in your travels, and I encourage you to reach out to Matthew. He's a beautiful person.

New story

I went out today and I noticed three girls as I got off the train. I discerned that they were witches, and of course I was attracted to them once again. I'm attracted not only to females but to their power. I was sitting and waiting to meet a friend for dinner, and one of the prettier ones started talking to me (she astral travelled to me). I said, "I have a friend called Gamiel. He's an angel who's going to take you back to where you come from. The only way you can continue conversation with me isn't by astral traveling to me. It's time to come and meet me in the flesh. If you're not prepared to meet me in the flesh and have a conversation, you're not welcome."

Gamiel took her back to where she came from. I'm still not aware of how this girl went off into a shopping center and went the opposite way to myself. I'm not aware of how they can find me. But she came directly to me by astral travel, so Gamiel took her back.

Gamiel is running really good interference and protecting me from witchcraft. It seems that every young witch thinks the best card they can play is to try to seduce me and start some sort of relationship with me. Many of them have tried that angle to start with, except the one in the post office; she just tried to destroy me. I just wanted to add this part and say that it's really good to have an angel to run interference on them. I'm not sure how I'd be coping, or whether I'd be coping if I didn't have an angel protecting me and stopping them from contacting me.

I'm happy with heaven playing the middleman between me and other people. Gamiel actually told me today when I saw the three girls that they were witches, and I was attracted to them because they were sending something from themselves, especially the little one and the one that came to chase me up. So, I hope that's been informative to you. It's a terrific thing to be led and directed by angels.

Postscript

Over the months that have passed since I recorded the videos for this book, Katrina the witch has become a good friend. She often visits me in my house and is here as I edit the information about her at 7 a.m. this morning. I know she is on God's side because Gamiel allows her to come into my house.

Important contact

You can contact Auty, who has been mentioned many times in this book, for prophetic services, life coaching and counseling at https://gloryrealm777.com.

Closing thoughts

Sometimes we need more than words on a page to make a proper judgement. Things can be misunderstood and misinterpreted by simply reading text. The world has 40,000 separate denominations of the church based on the foundation of one book—the Bible.

With this in mind, what I have told you in this book could be misunderstood, judged, scoffed at and rejected by many people. The fact I have not seasoned my book with scripture verses to back up my stories might cause even more alarm. Many people after reading this will have an uneasy feeling that might never go away. That is demonic, and something in this book caused that reaction in you.

I don't confess to be a person without sin and free of error, but Auty watched the video that this book came from. If you can, find the video called *How You Can Minister with Angels in an Effective, Ongoing and Lasting Way.* You will notice a comment from Fire in the Spirit Ministries, which is Auty's YouTube channel, and he said *"Love it, Mate! Good job!"* I have tried my best to make a good book here and explain how I work with angels. It's my intention in this book to encourage you, inspire you and teach you some things.

I can't say that many of you will ever encounter Michael the Archangel or any archangel on Earth, and I didn't share these stories to boast or do so in any prideful way. You will find if you read my books that I am very transparent and just as honest with my frailties and failures and sins as I am with great successes and strengths. Above all things, seek intimacy with Jesus.

Go strong and prosper! (Joshua 1:7)

Love,

Matthew Robert Payne

January 2021

I'd Love to Hear from You

One of the ways that you can bless me as a writer is by writing an honest and candid review of my book on Amazon where you purchased this book. I always read the reviews of my books, and I would love to hear what you have to say about this one.

Before I buy a book, I read the reviews first. You can make an informed decision about a book when you have read enough honest reviews from readers. One way to help me sell this book and to give me positive feedback is by writing a review for me. It doesn't cost you a thing but helps me and the future readers of this book enormously.

To request a life-coaching session, request your own personal prophecy, or receive a personal message from your angel, you can also visit my website at http://personal-prophecy-today.com. All of the funds raised through my ministry website will go toward the books that I write and self-publish. To read up to 40 free books by me you can visit https://matthewrobertpayne.com

To write to me about this book or to share any other thoughts, please feel free to contact me at my personal email address at survivors.sanctuary@gmail.com.

You can also friend request me on Facebook at Matthew Robert Payne. Please send me a message if we have no friends in common, as a lot of scammers now send me friend requests..

You can also do me a huge favor and share this book on Facebook as a recommended book to read. This will help me and other readers.

Please do not be afraid to contact me and connect with me. I enjoy speaking my readers and all my best friends have read most of my books over time. I can't contact you as I don't know who you are, but you can contact me ☺

How to Sponsor a Book Project

If you have been blessed by this book, you might consider sponsoring a book for me. It normally costs me at least $1,200 to $1500 to produce each book that I write, depending on the length of the book.

If you seek the Holy Spirit about financing a book for me, I know that the Lord would be eternally grateful to you. Consider how much this book has blessed you, and then think of hundreds or even thousands of people who would be blessed by a book of mine. As you are probably aware, the vast majority of my e-books are ninety-nine cents, which proves to you that book writing is indeed a ministry for me and not a money-making venture. I would be very happy if you supported me in this.

If you have any questions for me or if you want to know what projects I am currently working on that your money might finance, you can write to me at survivors.sanctuary@gmail.com and ask me for more information. I would be pleased to give you additional details about my projects. I have currently 5 books that I need funds to publish.

You can sow any amount to my ministry by simply sending me money via the PayPal link at this address: http://personal-prophecy-today.com/support-my-ministry.

You can be sure that your support, no matter the amount, will be used for the publishing of helpful Christian books for people to read.

About Matthew Robert Payne

Matthew Robert Payne, a teacher and prophet, enjoys writing what the Lord puts on his heart to share. He receives great pleasure from interacting with others on Facebook, hearing from people who have read his books, and prophesying over people's lives. He is a passionate lover of and disciple of Jesus Christ. He hopes that as you discover his books, you will intimately come to know Jesus, the Father, and Matthew through his transparent writing style.

Matthew grew up in a traditional Baptist church and gave his heart to Jesus Christ at the tender age of eight years old. But he left home at the age of eighteen, living a wild life for many years and engaging in bad habits and addictions. At twenty-seven, he was baptized in water and, at the same time, baptized in the Holy Spirit. Matthew learned about the five-fold ministry offices and received a revelation of their value today.

He started his journey as a prophet twenty years ago, learning about this gift and putting it into practice. With thousands of prophecies under his belt, he can confidently prophesy to friends and strangers alike. He has been writing for a number of years and self-published his first book in 2011. Today he spends his time earning money to self-publish and writes many books as often. He also produces many videos that you can view on YouTube.

You can connect with him on Facebook. You can sow into his book-writing ministry, receive a message from your angel, or even receive your own nine-minute personal prophecy from Matthew at http://personal-prophecy-today.com.

Acknowledgments

I want to thank Jesus, the Holy Spirit, the Father, my scribe angel Bethany for the knowledge and wisdom in this book. I live to write books.

I want to thank my friends Mary, Shayne, Dundy, Lisa and others who support me with their love. Your love is priceless to me, a broken man.

I want to thank everyone else who has been used to encourage me and support me in friendship, prayer and finances. I want to especially thank those who choose to make a monthly support to my ministry and John who makes a donation every 2 weeks. This really helps me.

Printed in the USA
CPSIA information can be obtained
at www.ICGtesting.com
LVHW050555150224
771724LV00014B/826